# HOME ART

### Creating Romance and Magic with Everyday Objects

# Judyth van Amringe

### Photographs by Andrew Garn / Foreword by Marilyn Bethany

A Bulfinch Press Book • Little, Brown and Company • Boston • New York • Toronto • London

Thanks to Glenn Helmers for putting the text into English.

LIBRARY OF CONGRESS CATALOGING-IN-PUBLICATION DATA

van Amringe, Judyth.
    Home art : creating romance and magic with everyday objects / Judyth van Amringe ;
    photographs by Andrew Garn. — 1st ed.
        p.   cm.
    "A Bulfinch Press book."
    ISBN 0-8212-2068-3
    1. Furniture finishing.  2. Upholstered furniture — Repairing.  3. House furnishings.
4. Lampshades.  5. Decoration and ornament.   I.  Title.
TT199.V36   1994
749 — dc20                                                          93-48003

Designed by Jeanne Abboud

Bulfinch Press is an imprint and trademark of Little, Brown and Company (Inc.)

Published simultaneously in Canada by Little, Brown & Company (Canada) Limited

PRINTED IN HONG KONG

for my brother Jon —
+ my best pals —
Bix + Ruby
X X X

# CONTENTS

# FOREWORD

If, on the other hand, you have had it up to here with restraint, reserve, and reverence, this is the book for you. But first, a word about its author.

Judyth van Amringe is to the world of handicrafts what Charlie Parker was to the world of jazz — its hippest practitioner. Like all hip people, Judyth can be rather strange and intense. Which is not to say that she isn't excellent company. (Can the woman who had the wit to stencil a kitchen wall with "When the moon hitsa your eye like a bigga pizza pie" be anything but amusing? I ask you.) But Judyth most emphatically is not just one of the girls. She's intensely private, not especially eager to please, and markedly weak in the gossip department. More to the point, she'd rather get up at four A.M. to go to a flea market by herself than get dressed up to attend a gala event. But those of us who know and love Judyth have learned to overlook these eccentricities. We understand that she is saving herself for a higher calling — the consuming enterprise to which she has presently dedicated herself. It consists of accumulating the sort of doodads that slip through other people's fingers and attaching them to unlikely household objects in a manner so breathtakingly original (and at times downright subversive) that the results challenge conventional barriers between art and craft.

To her friends and fans, Judyth van Amringe is a woman warrior armed with a hot glue gun. But touchingly, Judyth doesn't see herself that way at all. She views her work as almost regular, just prettier. She seems to think that, by taking the rest of us by the hand, we'll be able to get to where she is, if we'll only take the time and trouble. Personally, I have my doubts. Nonetheless, I plan to follow wherever she leads with this book. If past experience is any indication, I may not end up in Judyth's realm, but I also won't end up where I started. Which is certainly the point of books and maybe even life.

— MARILYN BETHANY

# INTRODUCTION

**B**ring on the color! I think color is one of the most joyful and important elements of life. It informs every bit of the world around you — you just need to see it. In this book I hope you will learn to love color as deeply and disrespectfully as I do — to use it with pure abandon — not to be afraid of it but to immerse yourself in it until you're dizzy. Put your preconceptions of what should and shouldn't go together away — do exactly the opposite of what your old sense would tell you and you will find yourself in a whole new creative landscape. Believe me, it will work.

The other important factor in making home art is recycling. We all know how much appalling waste goes on all around us every day. My credo is to re-use as much stuff as possible always — whether it's mine, my neighbor's, something from a tag sale, a flea market, the street — because if you make something wonderful out of a cast-off you are saving its energy and making a little less clutter. Here is the challenge: to turn a piece around, rework it, make it totally your own, your style, your signature.

Amass lots of things. Collect odds and ends you respond to because when you need them, if you haven't collected them — they won't be there to use! Be open to the little bits of history available in

flea markets and tag sales — button boxes and hand-tied rugs, needlework pillow covers and hat trimmings all possess the mystery and weight of the past and will make your recycled home art magical. Don't worry if you get home with a carload and think, "Why did I buy all this stuff?" You will use all or part of these things to invent new objects.

A few practical words about where you will make your home art and where it will live. You will be making intense and intricate conversation pieces as you use this book, and your walls, optimally, should be a smooth envelope for the objects contained within them. I like creamy white or — true to form — deep, vibrant hues that don't look washed out against all the exuberant color I use on the furnishings. In my opinion, walls are there to hold things up. A small wall space can be accentuated by covering it almost completely with a bunch of something — say, empty picture frames. The opposite is also true: a large wall can be dramatized by hanging one beautiful item on it, such as the Macaroni Seashell Mirror (page 89) or the Rose Picture Frame (page 93). If you like, you can paint a door or window molding to tie in with what you're doing in the room.

Your work space can be described very easily: it should be comfortable for you. I have found it most comfortable to work on lamps standing up, decorating the shades at eye level. But you can also put a large shade over your knee and sew away at it while seated in a cozy chair. Big pieces like a couch require constant circling on foot, exacting bead work needs good lighting and some distraction — like music or TV. Just make sure that your hands and eyes have easy access to the object you're working on, and that your back is not strained or twisted in any way.

If you have a comfortable work space, get ready to dig out your cupboards, scavenge some beads, buttons, ribbons, and oddities, and make some home art.

# SOFAS · CHAIRS · OTTOMANS

## What to look for:

Just about any sofa, upholstered chair, or ottoman — no matter how down-and-out it may appear — can be transformed into something marvelous with a slipcover and a little elbow grease and ingenuity. Look for sturdy, shapely pieces in reasonably good condition. Minor problems can be easily fixed. If the springs are falling out of the seat bottom, simply bind them back in with burlap tape, usually available from an upholstery shop or supplier. If the black fabric that typically covers the seat bottom and springs is torn, remove it and tack on a new piece of fabric. It certainly doesn't have to be black! The remedy for a less-than-super-comfortable foam rubber cushion is to have a down one made to replace it. As for a feather cushion that has lost its loft due to age, the same pillow renovator (you can usually find one in the yellow pages) can restuff it for you. Torn fabric on a sofa, chair, or ottoman can be patched with a remnant, because once the slipcover is on, you won't notice it.

I especially like wing chairs and big club chairs because they look friendly and inviting, and they are almost always comfortable. Good feet on a chair or ottoman are appealing — just like a fabulous shoe that slips out from under a long skirt. They are almost always beat-up, but this can easily be concealed with silver or gold leaf or a coat of bright-colored paint.

## Slipcovers and fabric:

If you are an expert and know how to make your own slip-covers, I commend you —

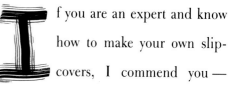

just do it whenever a slipcover is called for. All others should scan the yellow pages — there will certainly be entries under upholsterers. Unless I am using vintage fabrics for my slipcovers, I generally stick to the same heavy (suiting-weight) linen, either in black or off-white, and the same black cotton brush fringe. They are rich in texture, and the linen is somewhat similar to the canvas that artists paint on. The reappearance of these materials also helps tie a room together, even when the surface decoration is quite different. Natural fabrics are ideal for the slipcovers needed in the following projects because they let the inks

soak in. Synthetic fabrics are okay if you use acrylic paint rather than ink, but you have to water down the acrylic so it won't crack. A fabric with a jacquard pattern is a nice alternative to linen because its woven pattern adds another dimension to the painting.

## Paints:

In almost every project that involves painting in this book, I use Winsor & Newton Liquid Acrylic Colour. This is a brand of ink, not acrylic paint, for use with airbrushes, technical pens, brushes, and pens, and it comes in jars of one fluid ounce. I like it because it is thin in consistency, transparent, waterproof, and colorfast. For all of these reasons, the color is more luminous and brighter than acrylic tube paints, which are mixed with heavier pigments, giving them a different consistency and making them opaque to some degree. Winsor & Newton inks are not bad for your skin, nor are they noxious, but the fastidious may want to use the thin rubber gloves (similar to those used by surgeons) that are available in most paint and craft stores. Thicker rubber gloves will make you clumsy. Alternatives to Winsor & Newton are other brands of ink as well as acrylic paints. Sometimes I use fabric paint, on the Pollock Chair and the lizards for the Fish-and-Flower Screen. It is opaque and shows up better on dark-colored fabrics where the inks would disappear. ◪

# The Painted Sofa

## What you will need:

- ▣ Sofa
- ▣ Linen for slipcover
- ▣ Black 2-inch cotton brush fringe
- ▣ Lace, ribbon and rhinestones for skirt
- ▣ Newspaper
- ▣ Winsor & Newton Liquid Acrylic Colours (assorted tints)
- ▣ Water
- ▣ Jars or small containers for inks
- ▣ Paintbrushes, assorted sizes 5–12, round-tip, for acrylics

## How to make it:

**M**y sofa had been telling me to redo it almost from the minute it was delivered years ago. I had supplied the olive-green gabardine fabric, but the upholsterer had used plastic thread, which I hate. As a result, I kept the sofa perpetually draped with blankets and pillows. For the rehab, I chose neutral off-white linen slipcovers and had new down-and-feather cushions made, a plush 8 inches thick, so that the sofa would be a favorite sleeping place for my poodle, Ruby. The black fringe along the seams gives the sofa a real lift. (If you are sewing it yourself, sandwich it into the seams instead of using normal welting; then pull the thread that holds the fringe together on the outside edge and it will spring free. If you're having the slipcover made, the professional will know exactly what to do.) I embellished the slipcover's skirt with an apron of handmade lace (you could almost call it a slip) that I found at

a flea market. For some color, I wove a green grosgrain ribbon through the top and sewed on blue rhinestones, then sewed on the whole thing to the top edge of the slipcover skirt with a running stitch. You could just as easily make a little overskirt with wide ribbon or a beaded fringe of your own making — basically just about anything that adds a little lively detail.

The sofa's new off-white linen slipcover presented me with a clean canvas for painting. I wanted an abstract, freeform design with lots of buoyant color anchored by tracings of black to echo the furry cotton fringe. A good rule of thumb is to start on the back. This way any mistakes you make won't be as noticeable in the end (everyone needs to warm up), and you can experiment a bit with your design. Before you begin, it's a good idea to lay down newspaper on the floor around where you will be working.

I usually create an outline pattern with the black ink and then color in, adding a few more black brush strokes at

the end. Dilute the Winsor & Newton inks one to one in wide-mouthed jars or containers. Don't be afraid of drips, which I always make on purpose anyway. Drips make it look hand-done, which is definitely the idea here. With this project, I started out doing curlicues on the seat back, but I discovered my design was tighter and more rigid than I really wanted. I loosened the design up on the rest of the sofa, creating a checkerboard of circles and grids.

The beauty of this sofa is that if it gets dirty or stained, you just paint right over it. And the eyes on the back of the couch will watch out for trespassers! ◨

# The Jackson Pollock Chair

## What you will need:

- Chair
- Black linen for slipcover
- Black 2-inch cotton brush fringe
- Newspaper
- White iridescent fabric paint, Texticolor by Sennelier or Deka Permanent Fabric Paint brand
- Paintbrushes, size 12, round-tip, for acrylics
- Winsor & Newton Liquid Acrylic Colours (assorted tints)
- Jars or small containers for inks

## How to make it:

Fans of Jackson Pollock's spattered paintings will enjoy this simple project. Start with a black linen slipcover with black cotton fringe for your chair. Mine is a friendly old wing chair (any style will do). Ignore the pile of chiffon braid on the chair; we'll use that on the Chiffon Ottoman. I had the slipcover cut intentionally short to show off the wonderful claw-and-ball feet. Cover the floor well around the chair with newspaper; the spatters travel far.

Prime the canvas, so to speak, with an overall spattering of white iridescent fabric paint, flicking it on the slipcover, fringe included, with a brush. The paint on the fringe, which you can't really avoid anyway, is just a sign that the

chair is one of a kind and hand-done. Let the fabric paint dry, which takes a couple of hours, so that the Winsor & Newton inks won't bleed onto it. Empty these colors into separate wide-mouthed jars or containers. (The brush won't fit into the original containers.) Flick on a succession of Winsor & Newton colors; I chose pink and green on the sides, orange, blue, and yellow on the front and back. If the Jackson Pollock style is not for you, you can paint gorgeous cabbage roses or polka dots and squiggles — whatever suits your eye and hand. With this chair, you really can't make a mistake — so go for it and have a good time. ◘

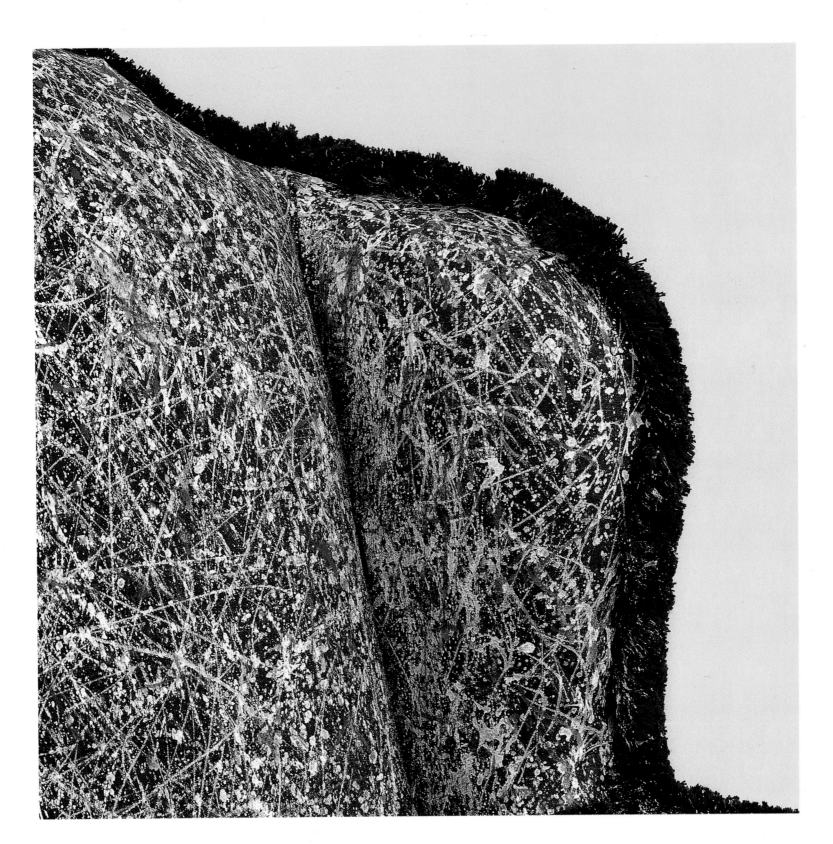

# The Pom-Pom Chair

## What you will need:

- Chair
- Old textiles for slipcover
- Black 2-inch cotton brush fringe
- Winsor & Newton Liquid Acrylic Colour (black)
- Paintbrush, size 5, round-tip, for acrylics
- Black 1½-inch acrylic pom-poms
- Glue gun
- 4-inch-wide ribbon, 2½ times the circumference of the chair base

## How to make it:

eautiful old textiles, bedspreads, and draperies don't have to be consigned to the chest in the attic. They can be reused in surprising new ways that their original makers would never have imagined. This is what I did when I transformed two pairs of vintage crewelwork curtains (a flea-market find) into the colorful slipcover for this black pigskin armchair — perfect for summer.

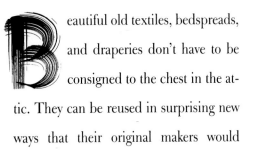

The luxurious texture of the crewelwork struck me as so wonderful that I decided to really play it up. I had the slipcover made with my favorite furry welting of cotton brush fringe and then I outlined the crewel design in black Winsor & Newton ink, both to draw attention to it and to tie it in with the black fringe. Next came the all-over smattering of black pom-poms, which I applied with the glue gun. (A note on this essential tool: it will make your life in crafts much, much easier. You can find glue guns in hardware stores, Kmarts, you name it. The only problem is keeping enough glue sticks on hand; I buy them by the 5-pound box.) At first I used small pom-poms but found them to be ditsy on such a large chair, so I quickly switched to the bigger size. The look is witty, almost clownlike — just right for an imposing armchair.

Cinching the slipcover at its waist is a 4-inch-wide piece of old lime green silk ribbon, finished with a fantastic bow at the back. (I feel the back of every object deserves equal embellishment.) You will need enough ribbon to wrap the base of the chair twice because the bow will require more length than you think, depending on the number of loops you make. I simply made three bows, one after the other, with the two ribbon tails. If the ribbon slips down on the chair, just sew it tight. The original reason for this silk belt was that the slipcover was cut a little too loose and didn't fit very well. It ended up being the perfect flourish for the chair. ◼

# The Beaded Slipper Chair

## What you will need:

- Chair
- Black fabric paint, Texticolor by Sennelier or Deka Permanent Fabric Paint brand
- Sponge brush, 2-inch
- Assorted fringe and beads
- Glue gun
- Other decorative add-ons: colored leaves, tiny rosettes
- Heavy-duty cotton thread, Hymark brand
- Needle
- Organza for skirt, 4 times the circumference of the chair base

## How to make it:

Improvise, improvise, improvise: that's always been my motto. Take it to heart, especially on a project like this one, where the same beads, fringe, and other embellishments would be virtually impossible to find, even if you wanted to copy it detail for detail. You want a similar effect, not an exact replica.

When I happened upon this delightful slipper chair in a Connecticut junk shop, it was painted to look like dark horsehair. I think perhaps, in its most recent life, it had been used as part of a theatrical stage set. Its shape charmed me, so I decided to fix it up. Step one was giving the already dark

surface two coats of black fabric paint (acrylic paint is fine too). Any chair that is tufted and upholstered in a smooth fabric will do.

Pull out any scraps of fringe, ribbon, and beads that you have accumulated. Collecting these items is a very good idea, because it is always when you need something that you can't find it. I began by edging the seat and chair back with an old silk fringe I had handy, attaching it in the crevices with the glue gun. I then crisscrossed the tufted seat and back and the chair's arms and top with tiny fabric leaves, again with hot glue. On the reverse side of the chair, I sewed on

six big starbursts from assorted beads; they almost look like sea anemones floating on the murky surface. The sewing is difficult on such a stiff, taut surface, so use a strong needle and a thimble. Try a big, bold design like this, which won't get lost on the relatively plain back of the chair.

My chair came with a scalloped flap over the skirt; you can easily substitute a length of long fringe. My favorite would be Victorian-style beaded lampshade fringe, 3 to 5 inches. The reason for this is to hide the unfinished top edge of the new skirt of silk organza (polyester if you like) that we are adding. To make this skirt flirty, take a length of fabric about twice the measurement of the chair base, fold it over width-wise, and iron 2-inch pleats into the fabric. Baste it together at the top and attach it underneath the flap of fabric (or fringe or beads) with a strip of hot glue. Doubling the

organza rather than hemming the bottom as well not only gives the skirt some weight, but it also results in a smoother look.

I embellished the scalloped flap on my chair with a crush of beads, dangles, and fabric rosettes, stitched and glued on in a pattern that echoes the scallop. If your chair doesn't have a similar feature, cover the unfinished top edge of the organza skirt with equally wild fringe, rhinestone appliqués, buttons, pearls, glass beads — you name it. Create a repeating pattern and run it around the chair just beneath the seat and covering the top of the flouncy new skirt. The more the better. ◙

# The Jeweled Chenille Ottoman

## What you will need:

- ☑ Ottoman
- ☑ Cotton or rayon chenille bedspread
- ☑ Assorted beads, appliqués, rhinestones
- ☑ Heavy-duty cotton thread, Hymark brand
- ☑ Needle
- ☑ Black ¼-inch acrylic pom-poms
- ☑ Glue gun

## How to make it:

This design also started from a vintage textile, this time from a bedspread I bought for $65 at a flea market. Aside from its glossy rayon yellow finish, the best part about the spread was its fabulous chenille medallion, so I cut out the center and had a round ottoman custom-made to fit. You can easily use an old ottoman and cut the cover to the right size. The slipcover, little more than the round chenille piece lined with the backing from the crewel curtains used to make the Pom-Pom Chair slipcover, I sewed myself, since there was none of the careful cutting re-

one you like. The clear yellow color of this coverlet called for rhinestones and other beads in bright, rich tones. Plan your design beforehand, laying out all your beads on a table. Start in the center, working your way around in circles — kind of like following the Yellow Brick Road. Not only does working from the center make the design easier to create, it also makes it somewhat easier to sew. Nonetheless, the slipcover gets extremely heavy as you progress. Be sure to double the thread and knot it three times on the back of the slipcover each time you start a new length of thread; the last thing you want is for the beads to come undone.

A few black pom-poms glue-gunned to the chenille patches at the base of the slipcover finish off the bottom edge and give it another texture. I also hung some big plastic crystal beads anchored with tiny jet beads along the edge. It is simple: just run the thread through the crystal bead, then through the jet bead, and double back through the crystal bead so you have a pendant. Repeat the process until you have circled the hem. The result of all this tedious handiwork is an exquisite ottoman so encrusted with gems that it is worthy of a princess (and yourself). ◙

quired for a more complicated piece of furniture.

The chenille medallion provided me with an instant pattern for sewing on beads: just fill in the empty spaces. This is true of any chenille pattern, so look for

# The Braided-Chiffon Ottoman

## What you will need:

- ◙ Ottoman

- ◙ Silver leaf, Italian, size 95 x 95 mm
  (25 leaves in an envelope, 20 envelopes to a box)

- ◙ Fast-drying size (15-minute), Easy Leaf Wunda-Size brand

- ◙ Sponge brush, 2-inch

- ◙ Black linen for slipcover

- ◙ Black 2-inch cotton brush fringe

- ◙ Silk or synthetic chiffon in 5 assorted colors, 6 yards each

- ◙ Heavy-duty cotton thread, Hymark brand

- ◙ Needle

- ◙ Rhinestones

- ◙ Pearls

## How to make it:

The neon colors and the twisting pattern of the braided chiffon just scream Pop Art and the sixties — not exactly what one expects from an ottoman. A beat-up ottoman with bun feet and yards of vivid chiffon left over from the days when I made scarves inspired this design. Any ottoman (or chair) will do for this project, but if it happens to have interesting feet like this one, why not make the most of them and silver-leaf them? I did that here (refer to pages 81–82 for detailed instructions) and had the black linen and cotton fringe slipcover cut short to reveal a bit of glimmering "leg" for added interest.

You will need to cut the chiffon into 3-inch-wide strips that are 3 yards long for plaiting. Use any extra you may have for the brim of a hat. Braid the chiffon by color — magenta, pink, purple, green, and blue — for maximum impact. If you like, mix one braid from the leftover colors of chiffon. Beginning in one corner of the top of the ottoman, sew on a braid in a tight circular fashion, tucking in the end pieces. Repeat with the rest of the braids, making sure to intertwine and overlap them for a three-dimensional impact. You can trail the tail of one braid over to the center of the next, or make a knot or a flamboyant twist. Just make sure you sew it down securely. Soon you will have a psychedelic fantasy of touchable, soft, woven chiffon. A few rhinestones and pearls stitched on (glue won't hold) to the plaiting only add to the magic. ◘

# ·TABLES·

## What to look for:

Tables come in all sizes and shapes: small, dainty occasional tables; low, long coffee tables; round pine tables perfect for dining. Some have drawers. Some have carved aprons. Others are very plain. Any table will do for the following projects as long as it's not too fancy or finely finished. I favor high tables, preferably those that are old and worn and of nice proportions.

## Sources

For some reason tables are some of the most easily scavenged objects of furniture I've come across over the years. People discard them all the time. So keep an eye out as you walk down the street — a treasure may be perched at the curbside.

Flea markets and tag sales are also natural places to find old tables, at very reasonable prices. And don't rule out the possibility of combining disparate elements: old wire spools or interesting pieces of driftwood or even gnarled old tree stumps make great bases, and a trusty slice of plywood will serve as a top.

## Structure

If you like the bones of a table, don't worry too much about the shape it's in. Obviously if it's worm-eaten or missing a leg or has signs of

dry rot you don't want to bother with it. But a wobble can easily be corrected with angle brackets, and if the surface is very warped you just have to glue your objects on so they don't fall off; see my Barnacle Table (p. 43) for inspiration. When the surface of the table is past saving, but the legs are sturdy and likable, I go to a lumberyard and get a good-sized piece of plywood to use as a top. Since it ends up covered with paint, lace, flowers, ribbons, and furbelows of all kinds, it really doesn't matter whether the top is fine wood or particle board. This type of "add on" tabletop can be a sort of moveable feast — switching from standard table height on top of a base to performing coffee table duty on top of a chest. The possibilities are endless.

## Surface

If the shape of a table is pleasing, I don't let a crusty, peeling surface bother me. Since I'm going to disguise it anyway, who needs perfection? To me, "alligatoring" of old paint or a few good cracks are signs of distinction. If your surface is radically chipped and peeling you should give it a rough scrub with some coarse sandpaper so it doesn't flake after you have painted it. And you can give it a coat of varnish at the end if you want a smooth finish or a tint over the paint you have used. I leave the degree of polish up to you.

# The Ivy-Covered Table

## What you will need:

- Table
- Milk paint
- Sponge brushes
- Winsor & Newton Liquid Acrylic Colour (ochre)
- Lace, about 1½ times the perimeter of the table
- Green grosgrain ⅛-inch-wide ribbon, same length as lace
- Rhinestones, blue and amethyst

- Heavy-duty cotton thread, Hymark brand
- Needle
- Glue gun
- Fake ivy (usually comes in bunches; about ½ bunch)
- 5 or 6 pieces of ¼-inch yellow rayon ribbon, approximately 18 inches each
- Imitation fruits or blossoms or leaves on wire stems

## How to make it:

I found this pine table outside a junk shop in Maine, its wood warped, cracked, and weathered to a rough patina. I instantly thought of decorating it with ivy because I could just imagine weeds growing through it in time. The store's proprietor thought I was a crazy New Yorker to pay $12 for what any self-respecting New Englander knew was a piece of junk. It just goes to show you that one person's trash is another person's treasure.

Take any old rustic table with dried-out paint and, using a sponge brush, cover it with milk paint, which a table

like this one would have originally had on it. I chose white because I wanted a whitewashed look, but milk paint also comes in a variety of lush, soft colors. After the paint had dried (about two hours, to be safe), I decided it looked too clean for my taste, so I sponge-brushed on a bottle of Winsor & Newton ochre, diluted one to six. The luminous color varies in strength from place to place on the table, which I really like. This is an effect you wouldn't get if you were to simply paint the table with yellow milk paint.

A fanciful apron for the table is easy to create. Find enough lace to wrap the tabletop about 1½ times, weave a long piece of green grosgrain ribbon through the openings in the top of the lace, gathering it slightly so the lace doesn't lie too flat, then stitch on a repeat of blue and amethyst rhinestones for color. Glue-gun the apron to the side edge of the tabletop.

Now for the naturalistic touches. Loosely cover the table with the fake ivy, both variegated and regular green,

wedging it into the cracks. If you don't have cracks in your table, nail the ivy down with tiny tacks. Twist a piece of ivy down one leg of the table, securing it with pieces of colored rayon ribbon. Tie on a few imitation fruits to the ivy, or if you prefer, glue on a few bugs or blossoms. I put my Green Sea Goddess Lamp (pp. 67–68) on top of this table, stuffing the cord through one of the cracks in the top. For a less noticeable cord, you could run it down the table leg with the twisted ivy. ◙

# The Gilded Parsons Table

## What you will need:

- Table
- Variegated imitation gold leaf
- Fast-drying size (15-minute), Easy Leaf Wunda-Size brand
- Natural sponge
- Silver leaf
- Winsor & Newton Liquid Acrylic Colours (olive green and ochre)
- Marine varnish
- Sponge brush

## How you make it:

This plain console table, gilded and painted for an underwater look, makes a simple base for an elaborate lamp or a favorite collection (like the glass fish shown here). To achieve this surface effect, gild the table or other object first with variegated gold leaf (see instructions for gilding on pp. 81–82), using a natural sponge to apply the size and leaving lots of empty spaces, then repeating the process with silver leaf to create a mottled effect. When you are happy with the gilding, dab on olive green Winsor & Newton with a sponge. After it is dry, apply splotches of ochre in the same intentionally uneven fashion. Because the gilded surface is a table, which will have to withstand lots of wear and tear, varnish the table using a sponge brush so that you won't see any brush tracks. Marine varnish, which has a hint of yellow to it, will give you a nice antique finish. ◙

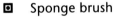

# The Barnacle Table

## What you will need:

- Table
- Black silk taffeta (6 times the circumference of table base) or 5-inch-wide satin ribbon
- Heavy-duty cotton thread, Hymark brand
- Needle
- Glue gun
- Tacks
- Lace
- Beads
- ½-inch black acrylic pom-poms
- A few or a lot of your favorite things
- 18-gauge wire

## How to make it:

This table is a very personal, idiosyncratic piece, decorated with an array of quirky objects — an ostrich egg, an alabaster heart, a Victorian change purse — that are meaningful to me for one reason or another. It is not especially functional, since I have glued almost all the objects to it, but I don't care. I love it and it reminds me of many happy times — what more do you want from a tabletop? If the idea of a table like this appeals to you, try creating your own personal assemblage with all those funny things you have hidden away in boxes and bureaus.

A plain table needs a skirt to lift it out of the ordinary. I folded over a 12-inch-

wide piece of black silk taffeta and gathered it with thread for a lush, generous skirt. An alternative to fabric is 5-inch-wide satin ribbon. Since I knew the skirt

would get knocked against, I attached it to the side edge of the top of my two-tone green oval table with a glue gun and a few tacks. I added a layer of unusual Czech wool-and-rayon lace from the 1930s — machine-made, geometric, and very colorful — that I had embellished with painted glass beads, also Czech but from the 1920s. These are things I had collected at flea markets over the years. A smattering of little black acrylic pom-poms glued onto the skirt give it the look of three-dimensional polka dots.

The base of my table was an empty shelf that needed to be filled, and naturally I complied, loading it up with crazy plastic beads that, glued en masse, resemble barnacles. I also glued on Victorian metal vases and a

big green Christmas ornament ball, itself embellished with tiny flowers, and some sand dollars and starfish that I had gilded.

For the top of the table, I created this lavish tangle of green beads within which I could set other objects loose (some are glued, some not). I strung the opaque Czech beads on 18-gauge wire so I could bend them and they would stay in the roiling functional nest I envisioned. My objects here range from three crystal balls and a box of Chinese fish made of bone to a piece of the Berlin Wall and a ceramic clam a friend made for me. I added a vase of sorts too — an ostrich egg I gilded, perfect for flowers. Since your table will no doubt be radically different from mine, the only tip I can offer is to mass the objects together as if you are building a sculpture. Add photographs, jewelry, rocks, or whatever.

At the very least your table will be a conversation piece. And you can always add to it or take away from it as time goes by. ◙

# LAMPS

## Lamp bases:

Finding good lamp bases is one of my never-ending projects. I like objects with worn patinas and interesting shapes — things that look as though they have had another life and are begging to be made both beautiful and useful again. That is why I usually have the most luck at flea markets, junk shops, and antique shows. There you can find wrought-iron floor lamps, oversized porcelain table lamps, and oddities such as the pair of mercury-glass magic balls that I used to make the Frog Lamps in this chapter. A useful tip: wrought-iron lamps often come with arms that can be removed for a more graceful line. Simply unscrew the finial from the top of the stand and replace

with a single bulb or cluster fitting. Large vases also lend themselves to being made into lamps. Unlike most lamps you will see in stores, mine are sculptures, illuminated focal points that look as good off as they do on. I recommend that you have all old bases rewired for safety. Another reason for doing this is that you may want to change the fixture; I often have a longer cord and a cluster of two bulbs installed, which lets me have the option of more light.

## Shades:

Matching a lamp base with a shade is just like choosing the right hat. My favorite shades are like Easter bonnets. Oppositions of size help create this "on parade" effect, such as a big, crazy shape wavering atop a stern iron standing stick base or a miniature shade on a gigantic base. It is the unexpected contrast that turns your eye. Whatever size and shape you decide on, be sure that the shade is unlined whenever possible because it is very hard to sew through

the air pocket between the shade and the lining. I also tend to choose silk shades over synthetic ones. Synthetic are perfectly okay since so much of the shades are covered with embellishments, but my feeling is that I spend so much time and energy on my designs that I don't want to compromise on quality. However, silk shades are expensive. I have often had my best luck picking them up at yard sales.

A dirty silk shade is easily cleaned up. Fill your sink or bathtub with Ivory Snow and water, dip in the shade, rinse in the shower (if necessary), and simply let it air-dry. When I have a shade with particularly bad stains to hide, I brush watered-down white (or a color of your choice) acrylic

paint all over it. One or both of these methods usually does the trick, but don't worry if the shade doesn't turn out spotless, because in the end, the aim is to gussy it up. That is why I will sometimes use a printed shade if it is all I have or if I want the texture of, say, a jacquard to be part of my design. And if there happens to be a small hole, just stuff a silk rose or a lace handkerchief or a scrunched-up piece of silk in it (make sure that it doesn't touch the bulb). No one will ever know but you.

## Electrical cords:

I adore the old-fashioned fabric-covered electrical cords that appliances and better lamps used to sport as tails. Nothing could be less charming than the rubberized plastic cords that are so ubiquitous today. My solution is to wrap them in one-inch-wide grosgrain ribbon. Black is my standard, but bright colors are nice, especially with dazzling shades, because they turn cords into stylish anchors. When you are having a

lamp rewired, be sure to have a generous 8- or 10-foot cord attached; you never know where you are going to plug the lamp in, and no one likes the look of an extension cord. Plus, once you have prettified your cord, you may want to wrap it around the base as a design element.

Start with the right amount of ribbon. The ribbon-to-cord ratio is an easy two to one, but you will also need extra for making bows. When in doubt, buy more, as you can use it on another project. (Buying more is my philosophy for everything.) To wrap the cord: Cut off one yard of ribbon (always with a diagonal snip so as not to waste any), tie one end to the top of the cord, hold the loose short piece with your

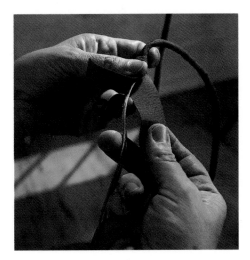

thumb, and cover it as you tightly twist the ribbon down the length of the cord. When this piece of ribbon runs out, take another yard-long ribbon strip and tie it in a knot over the first piece. Start again, repeating the earlier steps of twisting over these loose ends. Continue until you reach the plug; make a bow and snip off any extra ribbon. Now go back and hide the bulges in the cord (those places where you ran out of ribbon and started with a new piece) with big grosgrain bows.

Sometimes I will tuck in the stems of fabric leaves under the ribbon as I am wrapping the cord. If you use green grosgrain, the cord will resemble a trail of ivy or some other foliage. ◘

# The Where-to-Hide-Your-Jewelry Lamp

## What you will need:

- ▣ Lamp stand

- ▣ Unlined shade

- ▣ Fringe (enough to trim the shade's base)

- ▣ White glue, Sobo brand

- ▣ Assorted buttons and beads

- ▣ Heavy-duty cotton thread, Hymark brand

- ▣ Needle

- ▣ Winsor & Newton Liquid Acrylic Colours (black, blue)

- ▣ 2 brushes, size 3 for black, size 5 for blue,
  both round-tip, for acrylics

- ▣ Jewelry and other trinkets

## How to make it:

The theft of a box of my jewelry inspired this lamp, which is decorated with — you guessed it — some of my remaining pieces. Even before the burglary it had always seemed a shame to tuck my best jewelry out of sight somewhere, to be admired only on the few occasions I would actually get dressed up enough to wear it. Plus, my approach to design is really that more is always the best policy. The lamp is also a terrific place for broken necklaces and lonely earrings, mementos that you can't bring yourself to throw out. The idea is perfect for a bedside lamp, which is the place for sentimental, near-and-dear objects. But wherever you put such a lamp, damaged or pristine, fake or real, jewelry has the kind of glimmer and intricate detailing that lends itself perfectly to being illuminated.

I like a little fringe on just about every lamp. It harkens back to the days of those wonderfully embellished lamps of the Victorian era, long before the lamp became "lighting" and was summarily stripped of its rich decorative aspects. It also diffuses the light and can make a sultry shadow. With the white glue simply attach a length of fringe (any style and color you like) to the bottom edge of the shade. Now your lamp has a swingy coif of bangs.

Buttons and beads are my building blocks. They are shiny, and I like reflective surfaces of all kinds: rhinestones, mirrors, silver leaf. But because they can get expensive and I can't stand running out of anything, I try to buy my buttons and beads in bulk (see Sources, p. 115). You can do millions of interesting things with buttons, and you should always have enough variety and supply to mix and match with creative

abandon. Here I took a pile of round plastic black buttons (actually three different sizes) and sewed them onto the shade in tight groupings using doubled heavy-duty cotton thread. As I went along I occasionally embedded some purple and blue rhinestone buttons, which refract the light wonderfully, kind of like headlights on a car, within the black buttons. Don't be too rigid in your design. I treat the shade as a painting and just work with my mistakes

when I make them (which happen a lot more than you would ever think or notice).

Adding colorful brush strokes to the empty white spaces on your shade can add a whole other dimension. Try it if you like it. I used a square-edged brush to paint the shade's ribs blue and a skinny brush to paint the black chicken-scratch squiggles, which I think look a bit like the veiling you see on fancy hats.

The last step is really the frosting, which in this case turned out to be a few rhinestone-encrusted dominoes and lots of jewelry — the good, the bad, and the broken. I strung a piece of a broken necklace on with silver thread, attached a ring with a stickpin, clipped on many earrings (and pierced a few into the fabric as well). Remember that even if you don't love every single piece, the effect of them massed together in a collection is always more stunning. This is a rule I have found works with even the most mundane objects.

I love this lamp because it sparkles as much as a sky full of stars. And who needs a jewel box these days anyway? ◘

The Where-to-Hide-Your-Jewelry Lamp 53

# The Button Box Lamp

## What you will need:

- Lamp stand
- Unlined shade
- A big box of assorted buttons
- Heavy-duty cotton thread, Hymark brand
- Needle
- Silk dye (yellow), Vision Paint On Silk Dyes brand
- 1-inch-wide thick, floppy paintbrush
- Winsor & Newton Liquid Acrylic Colour (black)
- Brush, size 3, round-tip, for acrylics

## How to make it:

This lamp was prompted by my discovery of a big box of buttons, filled to the brim, at a flea market in Maine. A button-a-holic, I purchased the box and its contents on the spot for $5 — a steal since buttons have recently become a hot collectible in their own right. Undoubtedly the dealer could have multiplied his profit by sifting through the box in search of the truly special ones. But having all rare buttons isn't important to me, and it shouldn't be to you, because the approach I take with beads and buttons is always more, more, more. Just a few unusual buttons will look

especially gorgeous when set among a sea of ordinary ones. Also in the button box were an assortment of trinkets that had been tossed in over the years: garters, plastic prizes from gumball machines and cereal boxes, belt buckles, and even a button with the price tag still on. Like Minnie Pearl and her hat, I left the price tag on. The feathers are from my canary, Frank (Sinatra).

With this lamp, the idea is to create an overall "landscape" of texture through the repetition of buttons, be they boring brown or shiny-as-a-new-penny brass. Using doubled heavy-duty cotton thread, sew them onto the shade, one above the other, in a vaguely circular pattern. This will give the shade a most appealing three-dimensional aspect that just begs to be touched. For a zip of color I used red thread and stitched an X when the buttons had four holes instead of two. The plastic notions from the box make wonderful surprises, almost like punctuation marks. You could just as easily use more than one color of thread. I favor the bolder look of the heavier thread, but that doesn't mean you

can't recycle, say, the spools you might find in the button box or your old sewing basket. If the box is really old, the thread might even be silk or linen.

I like to fill in a shade's unembellished white spaces with a little detail. The color creates more of a landscape for the buttons, so that they don't just sit on the surface. Apply a swab of marigold-tinted silk dye with a big floppy brush. You don't need to use very much, as the dye bleeds wonderfully and the slightly uneven effect is more interesting than a flat coat of paint. After the dye has dried, take a skinny brush and black Winsor & Newton and add a few threadlike lines between the buttons. This kind of connect-the-dots scrawl visually ties the whole shade together. Button boxes are little collections of history. This lamp excavates these buttons from days when women darned, sewed, and mended, and saved particularly bright and beautiful buttons as treasures. While you make this lampshade think about where the buttons came from and what they might have been sewn onto. ▣

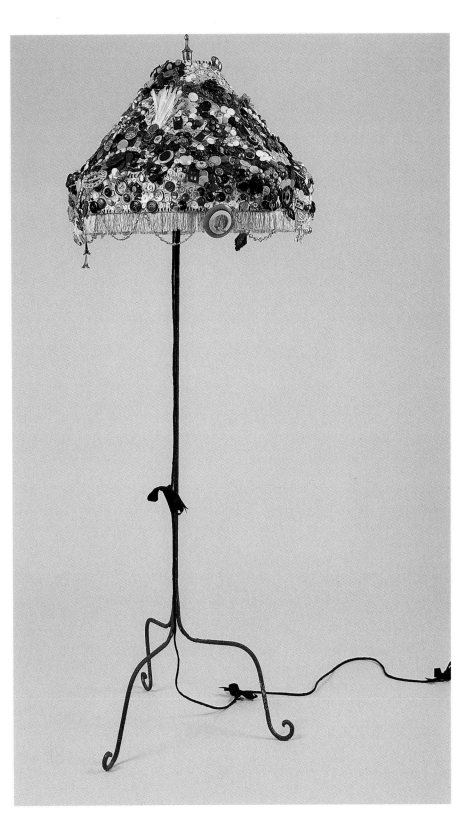

# The Silk Flower Lamp

## What you will need:

- Lamp stand
- Shade
- Silk dyes (yellow, green-gold), Vision Paint On Silk Dyes brand
- 1-inch-wide thick, floppy paintbrush
- Assorted rhinestones and appliqués
- Glue gun or heavy-duty cotton thread, Hymark brand
- Needle
- Assorted fringes
- Winsor & Newton Liquid Acrylic Colours (yellow, black)
- White glue, Sobo brand
- Silk flower petals in 3 different shades
- Large-eye sewing needle (if petals don't come with holes)

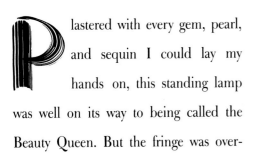

## How you make it:

Plastered with every gem, pearl, and sequin I could lay my hands on, this standing lamp was well on its way to being called the Beauty Queen. But the fringe was over-shadowed by the visual excitement above it, so I decided to add an exotic skirt of hot pink and orange petals. Now the lamp is more like a multicolored tropical drink with a big umbrella stuck in it.

Most white lampshades call out for a background wash of color. Sometimes I apply it first and other times as an after-thought to fill in the gaps of a particular design. Putting on the color afterward can

result in a more lively and three-dimensional look, thanks to the fact that not all the white gets covered up. But because you are going to just about cover the entire shade with beads, add the color here first. Swab on a light coat of silk dye with a big floppy brush. It will peek through the cracks later like morning rays of sunshine.

A lined silk shade, which I couldn't pass up at a flea market, prevented me from stitching on the assorted gems. If you have a lined shade and, like me, insist on using it, you can either sew the gemlike buttons, beads, and appliqués on (with great difficulty) or you can attach them with the glue gun, as I did here. Shoot out a short strip of glue and push the gems into it; too much

glue at once will get cold and the objects will not adhere as a result. Stop when you have run out of rhinestones and/or space.

A fancy flop of fringe is de rigueur with this lamp because of all the glitter. Tailored simplicity will simply not cut it. I used three different types of fringe: long, swingy fringe left plain; tassels, which I colored with yellow and black Winsor & Newton; and off-white fuzzy fringe, which I turned a greenish gold with a bottle of silk dye. Hold one hand (gloved in plastic) behind the fringe and stroke the dye on with a paintbrush. It will dry almost immediately. Use any combination of trimmings (as long as they are varied in style and length) and attach them with the white glue. I prefer

white glue to a glue gun in this case because the thick gobs of hot glue the glue gun dispenses make it harder to get the fringe to lie perfectly flat against the shade's surface. String the silk petals — hot pink, orange, yellow-orange — one by one through individual strands of the long fringe at intervals; if the petals don't come with holes, pierce them with a large sewing needle. Believe it or not, this Hawaiian lei-like skirt required 250 petals. In the interest of economy you can either skimp on petals, start with a smaller shade, or buy synthetic fabric petals. You could even use fabric flowers or take apart old corsages. However you do it, the effect will be gorgeous. ◨

# Twin Frog Lamps

## What you will need:

- One or two lamp bases

- Unlined shades

- Small plastic frogs (150), flies (50), spiders (25)

- Glue gun

- One large rubber spider

- Heavy-duty cotton thread, Hymark brand

- Needle

- Small pearl beads

- Black jet beads

- Metallic silver thread

## How you make it:

Remember those big mirrorlike balls that Victorians decorated their gardens with? A pair of mercury-glass bases, which I picked up at an antiques show somewhere and had rewired, inspired this lamp of creepy crawlies — a latter-day version of garden balls for your home. And what bug isn't attracted to a light source?

Any lamp base will do — a round, squat shape works well with these dunce-cap-shaped lampshades. Frogs, spiders, and flies make striking silhouettes on the off-white shades. If these creatures make you shudder, opt for sweeter friends from the yard, such as cheery ladybugs and butterflies. There are nearly 150 miniature frogs, mostly

black with a few navy and brown thrown in for variety's sake, and each with a set of glimmering rhinestone eyes. Using a glue gun, I covered the shades' surfaces equally with the frogs. Then I added about 50 plastic flies and 25 spiders, also with the glue gun, at random. A silly surprise on one of the shades: a single big rubber spider, which I had to sew on with silver thread because the glue wasn't strong enough to keep it from popping off.

Instead of a prefabricated flourish of fringe, I decided to devise my own with pearls, black jet beads, and silver strands of thread. Around the tops and bottoms of the shades I ran scalloped loops of tiny pearl beads, strung 7 to a scallop on doubled cotton thread, then attached to the edge with a stitch and repeated. Still not enough excitement, so I created another series of loops —18 tiny black beads strung onto silver thread — and dangled them from the loose pearl scal-

lops. The last element in this improvised trim turned out to be the short pieces of silver thread that I left hanging from the ends of the black bead loops. After tying the loop off, I left about 2 inches of silver thread to dangle. The whole thing rather reminds me of a fanciful spider web, especially with the silver thread. If you opt for ladybugs and butterflies, you may want to trim the lamp with silk rosettes (p. 94) or a length of dyed silk fringe (p. 60). ◙

# The Green Sea Goddess Lamp

## What you will need:

- Lamp base
- Unlined shade
- Silk dyes (yellow, olive, emerald, black), Vision Paint On Silk Dyes brand
- 1-inch-wide thick, floppy paintbrush
- Assorted fringe
- Cold-water fabric dye (olive green), BatiKit brand
- White glue, Sobo brand
- Assorted beads and appliqués, including pearls, glass ladybugs, green rhinestones
- Glue gun
- Heavy-duty cotton thread (black), Hymark brand
- Needle
- Black satin ribbon, ⅛-inch wide
- Metallic gold thread

## How you make it:

This dramatically oversized lamp caught my eye early one morning at a flea market. Its swollen green base is Chinese porcelain from the 1920s, and the shade it came with — rather reminiscent of a pagoda — was perfect. (You may not be so lucky. It is rare to find a lamp whose shade doesn't need changing; the proportions are usually all too predictable, and I never want anything to be predictable.)

The lustrous crackled green base called out for a soft palette of seaweed greens and yellows on the shade, originally dirty beige silk with no fringe. Your palette will naturally depend on the base you have found, but the approach will be similar to the one I am outlining here. The idea is to apply several washes of color, one after the other, so that they gently bleed together where they overlap — like you might see in a wa-

tercolor painting. This leads to an intentionally uneven, less flat look. Using a wide floppy brush and silk dyes, I applied golden yellow first, then olive, emerald, and finally cool black.

What makes this shade so appealing is the subtle layering of color, trims, and beads into a work of art that complements the base. Build up the three-dimensional aspect with whatever finery and techniques you like. I took some off-white short, fuzzy fringe, dyed it olive green, and attached it with white glue to the ribs and bottom edge of the shade. I almost always do an intentionally bad job dyeing the fringe so that the color will be irregular. The inconsistency gives the piece a handcrafted watercolor touch, which is such a great antidote to the machine-made plastic buttons and beads I often use. The next layer is composed of prefabricated yellow beaded "clumps" and white pearl "clumps." I believe they were originally intended to be made into earrings. (Because they have metal bases, I used the glue gun to

attach them.) They are scattered all over the shade, as are a bunch of white beaded appliqués. I sewed translucent green beads that I bought from a chandelier repairman into loose loops that meander across the shade's surface, and I attached short, wavering snippets of skinny black satin ribbon to the shade at their midpoint with green rhinestones.

Other embellishments include loops of tiny pearl beads and a handful of glass orange ladybugs I bought at a flea market. The little spots of bright orange really do the trick here, so don't be afraid to add a bit of sharp contrast when concocting your own shade. The last accoutrement was the trimming for the bottom edge of the shade: I applied a sweep of 3-inch-long fringe with white glue, then hung green glass drops, another flea-market find, from strands of shimmering gold thread. To me the lamp now seems like a lost treasure you might find under the sea, its shade an entwined mass of beautiful seaweed caught in a ray of sunshine. ▣

# Making a Wire-Mesh Shade

## What you will need:

- ▣ Metal shade frame
- ▣ 18-gauge brass or copper wire
- ▣ Wire cutters

## How you make it:

A shade that has so many tears, holes, and stains it appears to be beyond salvage doesn't necessarily have to wind up in the trash heap. If the scale and form of the shade are to your liking, it is a keeper. Just rip off the fabric and you are left with a metal frame to refashion into a new shade with a wire mesh. The old Victorian ones, if you can find them, have strange and wonderful silhouettes.

Building a wire mesh over the metal frame is easy. Cut a piece of 18-gauge brass or copper wire long enough to extend vertically from the top to the bottom of the frame, tie it off at each end, and repeat at regular intervals of ¾ to 1 inch around the frame. Construct the horizontal part of the mesh by weaving wire pieces through the vertical ones and tying them off at the end. The result is a basketlike mesh that is not only beautiful in its own right but also strong enough to keep all kinds of decorations from falling into the bulb and causing a fire. It can be embellished in myriad ways. Two of my favorite designs are the Fruit Lamp and the Christmas Ornament Lamp that follow. ▣

# The Fruit Lamp

## What you will need:

- Lamp stand
- Wire-mesh shade frame
- Plastic fruit hat trim
- Metallic gold thread
- Needle
- Turquoise and crystal beads

## How you make it:

You can put just about anything onto the wire-mesh frame. Strips of plastic fruit made for decorating hats form a wonderful wig, but you could just as easily attach fake ivy or vintage silk flowers or old corsages. Sew them on with strands of doubled gold thread, leaving metallic tails, and fully covering the mesh around the area of the bulb so that it isn't visible. Adorn any open spaces in the design with big rhinestones and beads, applied with doubled gold thread, and hang beads from the bottom of the shade on pieces 6 to 8 inches long. Again, keep the ends dangling loose for a desired wispiness. A little sparkle makes this lamp look good on and off. ◘

# The Christmas Ornament Lamp

## What you will need:

- Lamp stand
- Wire-mesh shade frame
- 18-gauge brass and/or copper wire
- White or off-white silk, about 18 yards
- Cold-water fabric dyes (6 assorted colors), BatiKit brand
- Heavy-duty cotton thread
- Needle
- Small Christmas tree balls
- Metallic gold thread

## How you make it:

All the colors of the rainbow can be found on this shade of silk rosettes and shiny Christmas balls. It could just as easily be a bouquet of overblown roselike pinks and reds or the more somber hues of foliage in the fall. The variations are endless. Try dangling any of your old holiday ornaments, mixing up the sizes, perhaps Mexican tin animals. Instead of silk swatches, you might use old handkerchiefs or scraps of lightweight fabric like gingham, treating the shade as you would a quilt.

Start with the same type of wire-mesh shades as called for on the Fruit Lamp

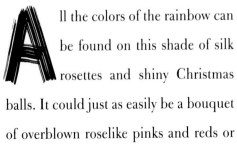

(p. 73). The fabric rosettes are 6-inch strips of shirtweight white or off-white silk (the width is determined by the width of the fabric, usually 36 to 54 inches). If you don't want the hassle of dyeing, buy remnants of colored silk; a mix of prints and solids can be beautiful. Color the 18 yards of silk in lots of 3 yards each with cold-water fabric dye, following the instructions on the package.

To make the rosettes: Fold the strips in half lengthwise, turn the long raw edges in about ¼ inch, and sew with doubled cotton thread, gathering tightly then tying off the thread. Complete the rosette by sewing the two unfinished ends together. The more rosettes you use, the lusher the shade will appear.

Slip a 3-inch piece of wire through the center of each rosette and, like a plastic bag tie, attach it to the wire-mesh frame with a twist.

The fringe on this shade is a ring of Christmas tree balls, hanging at different lengths from doubled gold thread. I prefer little balls to larger ones (they don't seem quite as Christmasy but are equally festive) and vintage balls to newer ones because of their attractive tarnished patina. You could always go for holiday glamour with a circle of just gold and silver. This lamp is a great year-round reminder that Christmas is right around the corner. ◘

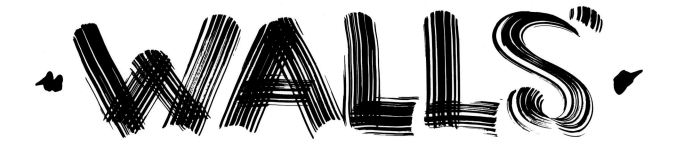

# "WALLS"

# Silver-Leafing

## What you will need:

- ◉ Silver leaf, Italian, 95 x 95 mm

  (25 leaves in an envelope, 20 envelopes to a box)

- ◉ 1 pint fast-drying size (15-minute),

  Easy Leaf Wunda-Size brand

- ◉ 2-inch sponge brush

- ◉ Varnish

## How to do it:

I have used the technique of gilding in all three of the projects in this chapter. Silver leaf is great-looking, especially after it has begun to tarnish with age. If you don't want to spend the time or money on silver-leafing, you can always cheat with metallic spray paint, but the result won't be as luscious and it will not tar-

nish. A less expensive — though no less time-consuming — alternative is aluminum leaf, though it doesn't share silver's luminosity or its tendency to tarnish. If you prefer gold to silver, try synthetic gold leaf (much cheaper than the real McCoy) or variegated gold, which has a "tie-dyed" appearance, with bits of blue, black, and red in the gold. Variegated

gold can impart a liveliness to a surface that might otherwise appear flat and even.

If you have never done any gilding, don't be intimidated; the process is not nearly as difficult as most people believe. Of course, any real gilder would be horrified by the way I do it. Begin by applying what is known as size (the adhesive)

to a small area of the surface to be gilded. Materials that are easily gilded are wood, glass, plaster — anything that the size will stick to. Be sure to use a sponge brush or a sponge, which won't leave visible brush marks in its wake, and size that is quick-drying, preferably 15-minute, rather than those more time-consuming varieties favored by the pros. The general rule of thumb is the longer it takes the size to dry, the more brilliant the gilded effect. Since I like things to look old and craggy, I don't want the leaf

to appear shiny and new. The finished gilded object should look as if it has been there for a hundred years. The quick size is milky white when wet, transparent when dry.

After you have sponged on the size, let the surface dry until it is tacky. Take a single leaf of silver from the package and rub it on with your hand. Proceed slowly, laying on leaf after leaf, because you don't want to waste such a precious ingredient. If you want a solid silvered surface, sponge-brush the size on evenly

and fit the squares closely. For a textured surface use a natural sponge and the silver won't stick where there's no size. If you would rather not have the silver eventually turn black, apply a coat of varnish or polyurethane after you have applied all the leaf, using the same kind of sponge brush. If you like a little tarnish, just hold off until the gilded surface has aged to your liking; varnishing at that point will stop any further tarnishing in its tracks. Varnishing also makes the surface easier to clean. ◪

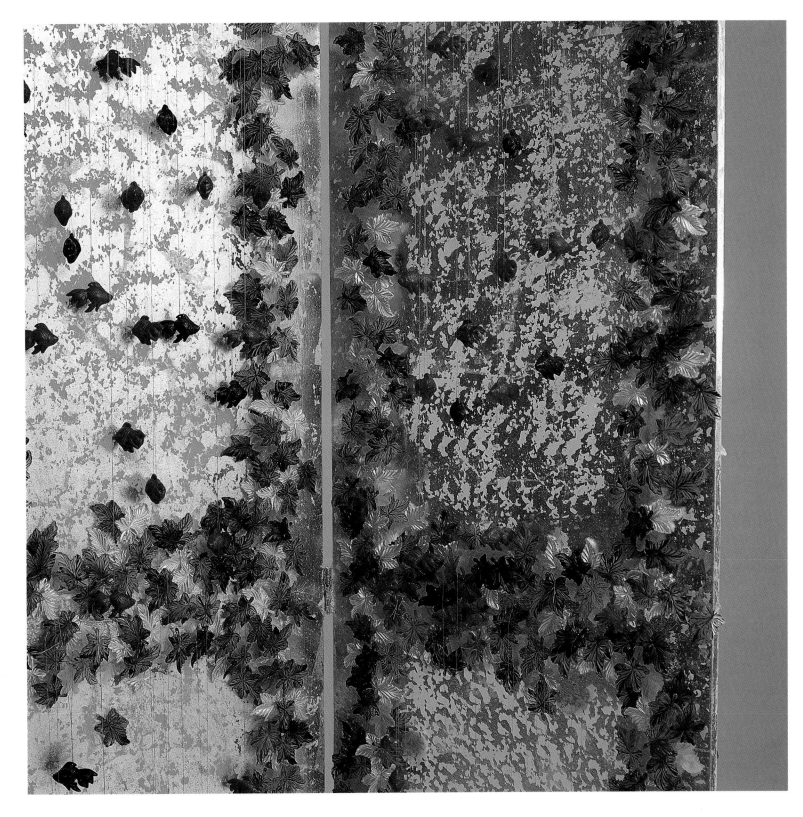

# The Translucent Fish-and-Flower Screen

## What you will need:

- Multipanel standing screen
- Fast-drying size (15-minute), Easy Leaf Wunda-Size brand
- Natural sponge, 3- to 4-inch piece
- Silver or aluminum leaf, about 1 box
- Fine sandpaper
- About 750 plastic leaves, opaque and frosted
- About 750 plastic flowers and pearlized leaves
- About 150 plastic frosted fish beads
- 12 yellow plastic butterflies
- 12 rubber lizards

- 2 rubber praying mantises
- Winsor & Newton Liquid Acrylic Colours (olive, emerald, sap green, ochre, black, orange)
- Several paintbrushes, size 6, round-tip, for acrylics
- Thin rubber gloves
- Glue gun
- Metallic silver thread
- Pearlized fabric paints (blue, pink, green, black), Texticolor by Sennelier or Deka Permanent Fabric Paint brand

## How you make it:

I started off this project with a five-panel screen featuring a wooden frame fitted with sheets of frosted glass. This is what I happened to have, but you could also decorate a wooden door with glass panes, a kitchen cupboard, or a bathroom mirror with a flock of flowers or a school of fish. What adds to the end result is the presence of glass, because its translucency when silver-leafed is magical, but wood works well too.

The first step is silver-leafing the glass panels on their frosted side. If your screen or door has plain glass, choose one side to gild; it does not matter which one. However, if you are working on a cabinet door, gild the inner side of the glass. To achieve the desired uneven, textured effect featured here, use a natural piece of sponge rather than a sponge brush. Dampen the sponge in water and squeeze it out so that it is supple but not water-logged, dip it into a shallow bowl of size, and dab it lightly onto the glass. When in doubt about quantity, err on the side of too little size because you want the sponge's holes to be visible. You can always go back and redo the places that didn't get amply covered. Proceed with the remaining steps of silver-leafing (p. 82). The nice thing about leafing is that spots you don't like can be fixed at any time during the process.

For the screen's wooden frame, which may be painted (mine was), the procedure is the same as above only if the surface is porous. If it is not porous, the size will not adhere. A simple test for porousness is to splash some water onto the surface; if the water beads up, it is not porous. In that case, you must sand down the frame with fine sandpaper and remove all the resulting dust particles before applying the size.

Once the silver-leafing of the screen's panels is complete, turn to your embellishments. I went to Manhattan's jewelry supply, millinery, and notions district and bought 750 plastic leaves, both opaque and frosted, as well as a total of 750 plastic flowers and pearlized leaves, 150 plastic goldfish, and a dozen plastic butterflies. Gear your quantities to the size of your screen. I needed a lot because I had five panels. The lizards and mantises I picked up at a little shop in

New York's East Village neighborhood. With an acrylic paintbrush and hands covered in thin rubber gloves, I painted the leaves in various natural tinted Winsor & Newton inks — olive, emerald, sap, and ochre (I went through two bottles of each color). I turned my plastic fish black and orange, like goldfish. These were my decorations for one side of the screen. I attached the leaves along the frame using a glue gun — not an easy feat because the screen is upright. Just press each leaf on and hold until glue hardens. I strung the fish with odd loops of silver thread and dangled them randomly from the tops of leaves for a goldfish-bowl effect.

For the other side of the screen, I chose a complementary gathering of the pearlized leaves, the plastic flowers, and the yellow plastic butterflies, plus a dozen rubber lizards and two rubber praying mantises. Again, I used an array of Winsor & Newton inks to color the leaves and flowers. I gave the flowers black-eyed Susan centers. The butter-

flies were just right the way they were. As with the leaves on the other side of the screen, I attached these little wonders with hot glue. The lizards I turned blue, pink, and green with spots of black, all in fabric paint, which sticks to rubber, something ink won't do. This way the lizards look like chameleons. I hung the

lizards and the pair of unpainted praying mantises from the flowers and leaves with the silver thread.

The finished screen shimmers like a reflecting pool — perfect for a sunroom and even better for a dreary city apartment where you want to be reminded that there is nature out there somewhere. ◨

# The Macaroni Seashell Mirror

## What you will need:

- Large framed mirror, preferably carved Victorian, with a generous frame
- Macaroni, various size shells
- Newspaper
- Metallic spray paint (gold, brass, copper)
- Pearlized fabric paint (green, blue, pink, peach, black), Texticolor by Sennelier or Deka Permanent Fabric Paint brand
- Paintbrush, size 6, round-tip, for acrylics

- Thin rubber gloves
- Silver or aluminum leaf, about ½ box
- Fast-drying size (15-minute), Easy Leaf Wunda-Size brand
- Sponge brush, 1- or 2-inch
- Lust R gild enamel leaflike-finish (optional)
- Silver spray paint (optional)
- Glue gun

## How you make it:

Macaroni makes great art: it is inexpensive, comes in a variety of wonderful shapes, and makes you feel like a child in play school again. This big beat-up mirror — with its lovely painted panel of roses and original beveled glass, slightly stained and tarnished — was an ideal candidate for a pasta redo. Macaroni, so three-dimensional, is perfect for hiding cracks and chips like the ones on this mirror's frame.

The 6-by-3-foot mirror required about 10 pounds of macaroni, so estimate accordingly — though, of course, I overdid it. Any unpainted extra can always be cooked for dinner. A mirror for a mermaid was what I had in mind for this project, so I bought lots of macaroni shells because they

resemble mollusks. I chose a combination of metallic spray paint and pearlized fabric paint to give the macaroni a sea-inspired iridescence.

Preparing the macaroni is relatively easy. The pieces to be spray-painted should be laid out on newspaper outside or in a well-ventilated room. After one coat, which dries almost immediately, turn them and spray the other sides. Don't worry if they aren't perfect; that's not the point. A longer and more painstaking process is painting the remaining pieces with fabric paint, which must be brushed on by hand. Lay the macaroni on newspaper and plunk yourself down in front of the television or turn up the stereo for a few hours of mindless distraction. Paint every size in a variety of colors because you don't know exactly what sizes and colors you will need. When you are in the midst of the creative process, the last thing you want to do is have to stop and paint more. The leftovers can always go on a small box or lampshade. Let the paint dry for about an

hour. Rubber gloves will protect your hands from staining (the paint isn't bad for your skin), but they can make you clumsier.

Now that the macaroni is glistening in its new radiant hues, tackle the surface treatment of the frame, which, in this case, I have made silver leaf. Silver suited my vision of this mirror in a mermaid's realm.

Estimate about how much of the frame you are going to cover in macaroni and buy the proportionate amount of silver leaf. Follow the instructions for silver-leafing on pp. 81–82. Of course, you can bypass this step and use either silver spray paint or brush-on enamel. Just bear in mind that these paints won't tarnish the way silver leaf does.

Attaching the painted macaroni to the now-gilded frame requires a glue gun and lots of glue sticks, as you are applying piece on top of piece on top of piece. A small dab simply won't do the trick. When a dollop of glue can be seen, just cover it with another pasta shell or paint over it. Hide cracks and crevices with macaroni, or accentuate them to build up peaks and valleys for a three-dimensional look. I even let some of the pasta wander onto the mirror itself, as mollusks will do. Try not to expose the inside of shell pieces because they will collect more dust this way. Even so, you will have to vacuum (with a soft brush attachment) the frame occasionally to keep it clean. ◘

# The Rose Picture Frame

## What you will need:

- Old frame
- Silver or aluminum leaf, about ½ box
- Fast-drying size (15-minute), Easy Leaf Wunda-Size brand
- Sponge brush, 1- or 2-inch
- 3 dozen white silk roses
- Silk dye (red, purple, olive green), Vision Paint On Silk Dye brand
- Newspaper
- Thin rubber gloves
- Sheet of plastic
- Glue gun

## How you make it:

I think picture frames are so great that I have decorated an entire wall of my New York loft with them. That they are empty only further accentuates their interesting shapes, carving, and interrelationships. I bought this 2-by-3-foot Victorian frame at a flea market for $25. It was gold with chipped plaster molding and already in need of rescuing. Then it fell off a windowsill in my loft and really got smashed up. Whenever I break something, I quickly turn it into something else decorative or useful in order to stop grieving about it.

Silver-leafing was my answer to the wonderful relief molding of the frame. The silvery glint is also especially nice here because the mirror is absent. The

the dye will stain counters and floors. I recommend rubber gloves for this one. Lay them on a sheet of plastic to dry for a couple of hours. With the glue gun in hand, attach the flowers around the edge of the frame, covering up any gaping holes or cracks. I tucked old postcards in among the flowers as well.

I left the old hanging wire strung across the back of the picture frame because I like the way it looks. Set it on top of a dresser or table and drape necklaces from the wire or use wooden clothespins to fasten old postcards (like I did) or snapshots. You can always leave the frame empty and let your imagination run free. ◨

tarnish of silver without varnish enhances the elaborate crevices, making the frame appear very sculptural, not flat-looking. Follow the instructions outlined in the silver-leafing section (pp. 81–82). Again, you may shortcut this step by brushing on silver enamel or spray-painting the surface.

A trim of silk roses helps hide some of the picture frame's damage as well as providing a soft, naturalistic decoration. I took 3 dozen white silk roses with green plastic stems (any flower will do) and dipped them like Easter eggs into bowls of red, purple, and olive-green silk dye. Put down plenty of newspaper because

# EXTRAS

# The Braided Hair-Extension Rug

## What you will need:

- A handcrafted rug — braided, hooked, or other
- Synthetic hair
- Crochet needle, size J
- Heavy-duty cotton thread, Hymark brand
- Needle

## How to make it:

I got the idea for this rug from a friend of mine, who wears her hair in the most incredible plaits, most of which are composed with ample portions of synthetic hair. Hair extensions, in the form of a fringe of braids, seemed like the perfect way to fix up this 1950s Scandinavian shag yarn rug. Their neon-bright colors really bring it to life. Any colorful rug with a handcrafted look, such as a braided or hooked rug, would do fine.

Synthetic hair comes straight and kinky and in a whole array of hues. Choose kinky because it holds the braid together better than the straight hair, and select the colors that complement those in your rug. Adding a fringe of braids to the edge of a rug demands little skill. Decide on how thick you want the braids to be and divide the hair into correct portions. Needless to say,

from the back to the side. Combine with the front half length, braid, and knot as with the other pieces.

Repeat this process to create the fringe, but don't make all the braids even — that is too monotonous. If a braid seems too long, knot it at a few intervals. And if the rug has holes in it like mine did, put a few scattered braids in the center to mend them. ◘

these do not have to be exactly equal. Start in the center of the rug. With a big crochet needle, puncture two holes about ½ inch apart through the rug and hook the length of hair all the way through and pull both pieces evenly to the front.

Then separate the combined hair into three pieces, braid, and knot at both the end and the beginning of the braid. When you get to the edges of the rug, make just one hole, hook the length halfway through, and pull the half length

# The Tiddlywink Pillow

## What you will need:

- Old pillow
- Ivory Snow
- Winsor & Newton Liquid Acrylic Colours (optional)
- Plastic tiddlywink beads
- Rhinestone stars
- Heavy-duty cotton thread
- Needle
- Embroidered doily or other embellishments
- Same size new pillow or stuffing

## How to make it:

 Old pillows can easily be reborn with a little ingenuity. This chenille pillow with its crewel-work design was lovely, but the edge was really boring — which most pillow edges

are. This flea-market find needed some gussying up, perhaps a new fringe. You can use any kind of pillowcase — one that has been cross-stitched, needlepointed, embroidered, you name it.

Begin by opening the pillow up along one of the seams and removing the stuffing (old pillows often get lumpy and can have a nasty smell). Wash the cover gently in Ivory Snow. If the colors bleed, go with

it; add a little design with some Winsor & Newton colors.

With your pillow cover clean and dry, start sewing. I stitched on masses of flat, round plastic beads in pastel colors, creating a wavelike frame for the crewelwork design on the front of the pillow. What is especially nice about the so-called tiddlywink beads is that they make noise when you move or touch the pillow. I also added black rhinestone stars for some sparkle. On the plain back of the pillow, I sewed on a colorful embroidered doily that I had lying around; its tassels stretch to fit the corners perfectly. Obviously, few people will have such an object handy. Try old lace or a cutwork handkerchief, dyed or painted, and tassel fringe, or paint a design on the empty canvas. This way you get two pillows out of one — double the pleasure. For this reason, I always make the back of an object as interesting as the front, no matter what it is. If you don't want to use tiddlywinks, colored fringe is a good alternative. You can dye it as described on p. 60 and welt it in. Or you could even sew loops of all different kinds of beads along all four sides (p. 64). If you do, be sure to use double-duty thread.

When you have finished fussing with the cover, insert a new pillow (down and feathers is my preference) and sew the seam closed. Now you have a decorative pillow that is both comfortable and as fun to play with as an old beanbag. ◙

# The Jacket Pillow

## What you will need:

- Decorated jacket or sweater
- Pillow for stuffing (preferably down and feather)
- Remnant piece of pretty fabric
- Heavy-duty cotton thread
- Needle
- String of fake pearls or other necklace
- Gloves
- Rhinestone pin

## How to make it:

This jacket was so stunning that I couldn't pass it up when I saw it one day shopping. Keep an eye out for such marvels, but also look in your closet for something similar — say, a beaded or sequined sweater that you haven't worn in years. Flea markets and vintage-clothing stores sometimes have perfect "pillowcase" items. Next find a new pillow (mine is square) that roughly fits the jacket. Sew a case for the pillow from a piece of pretty accent fabric like the blue-and-white polka-dot rayon I used. Put the jacket on over the pillow, fold the sleeves around the sides and to the front, tack them down with a needle and thread, and sew the bottom of the jacket together. If the neck has no fastener, tack the neck closing together at the front. Then pull a piece of the pillow through the neck opening and stitch it firmly so that it will stay out.

Accessorizing the pillow is the fun part. I made an ascot of the polka-dot fabric for the pillow's "neck" and entwined it with a string of fake pearls. Fancy white gloves and a rhinestone pin (which also helps keep the jacket front closed) complete this fashion statement. This project is especially great because you can express your personal sense of fashion and recycle those long-forgotten clothes in your closet at the same time. You could even create a pillow for everyone in your family using wardrobe cast-offs. Just make sure that the fabric is soft and supple, like all comfortable pillows should be.

# The Flamenco Television Cozy

## What you will need:

- Dress form, secondhand or new

- Black rayon taffeta, about 8 yards for underskirt

- Rayon taffeta in 6 colors, 2–7 yards each (the top flounce will take about 2 yards, the bottom, 7 yards)

- Sewing machine

- Polka-dot organza (or other petticoat fabric), 6 yards

- Needle and thread

- Two 10-foot pieces of 4-inch-wide ribbon

- Assorted rhinestones and beaded appliqués

- Glue gun

- Winsor & Newton Liquid Acrylic Colour (purple)

- Paintbrush, size 6, round-tip, for acrylics

- Sequin appliqués

- Metallic gold thread

- Postcards and straight pins

- Scarf (optional)

- Hat

# How to make it:

**D**ress forms, so like sculptures, offer wonderful possibilities for embellishment. I devised the Flamenco Television Cozy because I don't like seeing the TV set out all the time. The mannequin's big, flouncy skirt could easily be used for temporarily storing other items as well. For example, in a bedroom it would be a great spot for evening shoes, letting them peek out, or for the laundry basket.

You can buy dress forms secondhand in the garment district and often at sewing-machine repair shops. New ones can be purchased from retail suppliers (check the yellow pages), where they cost between $350 and $450. I prefer the secondhand dress forms because the muslin is usually yellowed, which I like, and they are cheaper. Most dress forms come on casters and can be adjusted up to about six feet tall. I like mine that way — larger than life.

The flounced taffeta skirt is composed of a black circle underskirt with a cascade

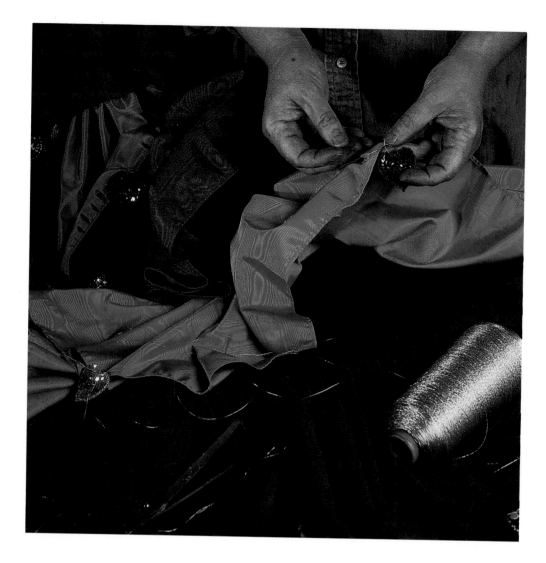

of overlapping flounces in dazzling flamenco-inspired colors. The bottom tier is polka-dot, which, in my mind, is synonymous with the costumes of these glamorous Spanish dancers. It's just not flamenco without polka-dots. If you are not an adept sewer, I suggest you go to a seamstress, who can make this skirt up easily.

To make it yourself, start by sewing a circle skirt from the black taffeta (use a pattern from a pattern book, since the skirt must be cut on the bias). The 7 flounces should each be 8 inches long; the top flounce requires about 2 yards of fabric, the bottom, about 7 yards. Baby-hem the fabric for each flounce on the sewing ma-

flounce is doubled (for ample lushness). You will not need to hem the flounce as a result.

The waistband gets finished off with a 4-inch-wide ribbon. I used one that I bought in Barcelona several years ago in a millinery shop. It sports the colors of the Spanish flag and is often worn in that country on holidays as a bandolier. I sewed two 10-foot-long strips of ribbon at their midpoints and attached them to the front center of the waistband for a luxurious sash. Wrap the ribbons once around the bodice and tie in the front for a huge double bow. You can easily imitate this look with ribbon of your own; combine stripes, plaids, or solids. The width and length are what make it luxurious.

Beaded appliqués and rhinestones, which I attached in a random fashion with a glue gun, adorn the bodice of this size-10 model. This form was badly stained. But you could dress it in a bustier or a flashy scarf instead. I filled in the bare spots of muslin with purple

chine. Gather the top edge of the fabric by hand to create the actual flounce. Do this for each of the 6 solid-color flounces, always checking that the amount of gathering on each flounce is equal and that the gathered flounce fits around the circle skirt at the appropriate height (there should be a 1-inch overlap from one flounce to the

next so that the gathered top edge is not visible). Stitch the top of the flounces onto the black underskirt using the sewing machine. This will also secure the gathering on the flounces.

Follow roughly the same procedure to create the bottom polka-dot flounce, but fold over the polka-dot fabric so that the

Winsor & Newton ink, so that the beads would not appear to be floating on top of the surface. The final flourishes include a smattering of sequin disks and hearts, which I sewed onto the skirt with gold thread; vintage Spanish postcards, which I pinned on; a gold-bead-encrusted bit of Victorian fabric at the neck; and a Mexican silver sombrero that I had been saving for an occasion just like this. A big, floppy straw hat would be appropriate too; just decorate it with ribbon, sequins, or flowers. ¡Olé! ◘

# SOURCES

**⊡ For general art/craft supplies:**

Pearl Paint
308 Canal Street
New York, NY 10013
212-431-7932

**⊡ For paintbrushes, marine varnish:**

Janovic Plaza
Long Island City, NY 11101
718-786-4444

**⊡ For lamps parts and rewiring old lamps:**

Grand Brass
221 Grand Street
New York, NY 10013
212-226-2567

**⊡ For Kamila linen suiting fabric (used on slipcovers):**

Hamilton Adams
104 West 40th Street
New York, NY 10018
212-221-0800

**⊡ For acrylic pom-poms, cotton sofa fringe:**

Conso Products Co.
P.O. Box 326
Union, SC 29379
803-427-9004

**⊡ For silk flowers, imitation fruits:**

Dulkin & Derrick
12 West 21st Street
New York, NY 10010
212-929-3615

**⊡ For rhinestones, beads (by the pound):**

Sheru Bead & Jewelry
49 West 38th Street
New York, NY 10018
212-730-0766

**⊡ For assorted beads:**

Mayer Imports
25 West 37th Street
New York, NY 10018
212-391-3830

Har-Mon Importing
16 West 37th Street
New York, NY 10018
212-947-1440

Ellis Import
44 West 37th Street
New York, NY 10018
212-947-6666

**⊡ For sequin appliqués, rhinestones:**

Fred Frankel & Sons
19 West 38th Street
New York, NY 10018
212-840-0810

**⊡ For fringes, beads:**

M & J Trimmings
1008 Sixth Avenue
New York, NY 10018
212-391-9072

**⊡ For glue guns and glue sticks in bulk:**

Gampel Supply Corp.
39 West 37th Street
New York, NY 10018
212-398-9222

**⊡ For metallic thread, antique notions:**

Tinsel Trading
47 West 38th Street
New York, NY 10018
212-730-1030

**⊡ For synthetic hair:**

Mona Trading Co.
956 Flatbush Avenue
Brooklyn, NY 11226
718-469-2214

**⊡ For ribbon:**

So-Good Inc.
28 West 38th Street
New York, NY 10018
212-398-0236

**⊡ For rubber flies and spiders:**

Little Rickie's
49½ First Avenue
New York, NY 10003
212-505-6457

**⊡ For gilding supplies (leaf, size):**

Sepp Leaf Products
New York, NY
212-683-2840
(wholesaler/must be called)

**⊡ For milk paint:**

The Old-Fashioned Milk Paint Co.
P.O. Box 22
Groton, MA 01450
508-448-6336